W9-ASN-952

BACKHOES
DIG!

by Beth Bence Reinke

BUMBA BOOKS™

LERNER PUBLICATIONS ◆ MINNEAPOLIS

Note to Educators:

Throughout this book, you'll find critical thinking questions. These can be used to engage young readers in thinking critically about the topic and in using the text and photos to do so.

Lerner Publications Company
A division of Lerner Publishing Group, Inc.
241 First Avenue North
Minneapolis, MN 55401 USA

For reading levels and more information, look up this title at www.lernerbooks.com.

Library of Congress Cataloging-in-Publication Data

The Cataloging-in-Publication Data for *Backhoes Dig!* is on file at the Library of Congress.
ISBN 978-1-5124-3355-5 (lib. bdg.)
ISBN 978-1-5124-5539-7 (pbk.)
ISBN 978-1-5124-5019-4 (EB pdf)

Manufactured in the United States of America
1—CG—7/15/17

Expand learning beyond the printed book. Download free, complementary educational resources for this book from our website, www.lernerresource.com.

Table of
Contents

Backhoes

Backhoes dig up dirt.

They carry and dump it too.

Backhoes work at

construction sites.

The digger bucket is at the back

of the backhoe.

It digs holes.

It dumps the dirt in piles.

The loader bucket is at the front.

It scoops dirt from the piles.

It carries the dirt away.

What else do you think the loader bucket could scoop?

An operator sits in the

cab between the buckets.

The seat spins.

It faces the bucket he

is using.

The backhoe has parts called

legs and arms.

Legs hold the backhoe steady

when it digs.

An arm moves the digger bucket.

arm

legs

13

This backhoe digs a deep hole.

It makes room for a swimming pool.

What else could a backhoe dig a hole for?

The digger bucket digs

a long trench.

Workers will put in pipes.

What other kinds of things do you think could go in a long trench?

The loader bucket scoops up dirt.

It will dump the dirt on top of the pipes.

Backhoes dig holes and scoop dirt.

They move dirt to do big jobs.

Parts of a Backhoe

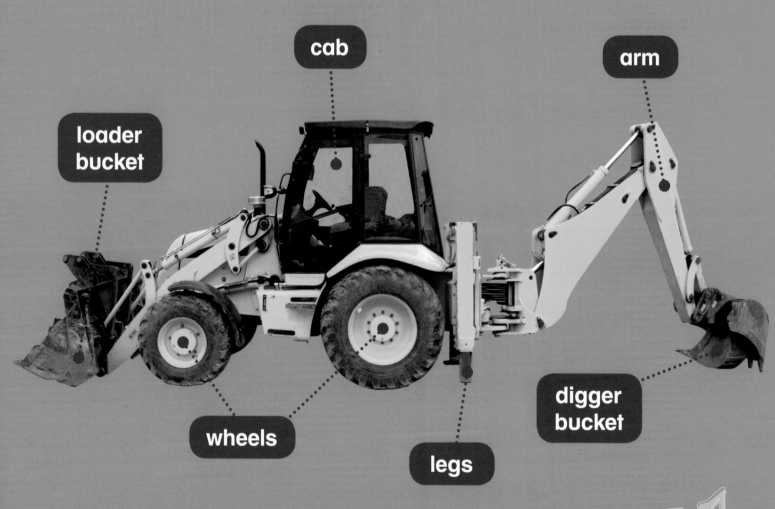

cab

arm

loader
bucket

wheels

legs

digger
bucket

Picture Glossary

construction sites

places where construction, or building, takes place

operator

the person who controls the backhoe

pipes

long, narrow tubes that carry water, steam, or gas

trench

a long, narrow ditch

Read More

Hill, Lee Sullivan. *Earthmovers on the Move.* Minneapolis: Lerner Publications, 2011.

Osier, Dan. *Backhoes.* New York: PowerKids, 2014.

Reinke, Beth Bence. *Dump Trucks Haul!* Minneapolis: Lerner Publications, 2018.

Index

Photo Credits